TWO FULL STOPS FROM GRAVITY

Poems by

Richard Atkinson

www.pretendgenius.com

Published simultaneously in the United States and
Great Britain in 2014 by Pretend Genius
978-0-9852133-5-0

Copyright © Richard Atkinson

To DAVE,

Better than
the DOGS

thanks to

Kim Göransson

for reading

Golden
Bollicks!
& Better
than the
REAL
thing!
cheers
Rich

poems

In Memoriam

Ruth Edith Atkinson (1924-2006)

Edith May Paice (Puddy) (1892-1984)

TWO FULL STOPS
FROM GRAVITY

at the flea market

hangover, dead-dog style,
sat, had a bacon butty and tea

watching someone buy
some beautiful yellow flowers.
it almost made me cry.

later saw a young girl with no arms
sit on the table

like an angry bored sculpture, cross-legged
behind a stall, selling nothing in particular

not in the pursuit of money,
just as a way of passing time.

really wanted to take her photograph,
but people would get the wrong idea.

she had her arms inside her
brightly-coloured anorak

her glum 'I'm so bored' expression
was a sight to witness.

big B flat minor talk

bird with crest, perched on tall grass beside
zephyr-swept clean reservoir, undulating.

sang a little and darted into undergrowth.
looking for something, anything
to make it tick, like you do.

its reed mate came by, crest-less, as small as a
B flat minor

looking for its partner.
pointed to where she should go.

B flat minor didn't take a jot of notice,
looking at me like I was insane.

must have understood humans want to destroy
things of beauty

hardly ever see, wanting only to attain things,
like we own them,
god and everything, even B flat minor.

as though we never hit the exit sign
lit up in smokey neon red
we were born to enter mostly half alive, dead.

had a chat with B flat, squeezing lips together
so they quivered, vibrated,
replying to her twitterings.

every time she made two, I made two, and so on.
we seemed to get along fine

even though
I could not sing as well as she could.

tiptoed, on top of strong silent type, grass,
shivering its nakedness in the snake breeze.

most intelligent conversation I ever had.
or will have.

B flat knew just about
everything there was to know,
secrets we had forgotten!

as smacked lips together, squeezing out chit chat,
a couple appeared

looking at me as if I had escaped from somewhere
they hide the keys from you.

B flat pretended she didn't know me, the creep
disappeared, without so much as a thank you

to find her partner,
and I had no one to talk to, again.

but the zephyr's breath felt fine and good,
and I had some left,
even inside the inside.

father dad jack

"why don't you call me Dad, son?"
betting slips "all bloody lost"

empty sherry bottles, fuse taken out of cheap record
player, plug.

to prevent fuss when drunk and
he wanted it loud, loud.

below him was a pensioner he described
as a living dead person
"miserable bugger" moan, moan, moan.

he helped out his unemployed mental health monk
drinking chum, only family he really had.

I visit, an Irish boozing friend is there.
dad played the tape I got him

The singing detective soundtrack. laugh!
I almost cried.

dad laughed as well, bellyache type,
thump thump thump on the armchair.

he said I'd be giggling about it later,
people would think me crazy.

the idea of dad sitting there with his boozing pal,
complaining about miserable buggers

while the corny tape played about
long lost sweethearts.

"no life ere!" "those bloody horses!"
"the bloody pools!" "those bloody tories!"

said whilst listening to old crooners talking about
their lost true loves, it really made me laugh.

dad gave me a bar of chocolate
at the end of the visit,
I gave him a little money for cigarettes.

in the hospital, we did not really speak.
he told me to keep warm up north,

still smoking like a factory.
"thought me back had gone"

dad was half dead,
riddled with cancer, life out of eyes,
still moaning "theirs no bloody life ere!"

watching the footie whilst moaning about
Charlton's coaching skills.

on crutches, he fell on the way to the toilet,
would not let me help him back up,
he died soon after.

it took many visits to the doctor
before they felt the obvious lumps,
under his arm pits, he was full of it.

no one wants to touch a dirty old man,
the barstools.

"don't let the barstools get you down son"
yes Jack…sorry Dad.

black lace

we sat opposite each other
do you believe in god she says

well there must be one
but only shows herself when drunk
and at end of tether like most of the time
and has a sense of humour and pain

how long have you been afflicted she says
hell, I don't know I say, it's always happening to me
like something stuck in the head
that needs to come out

do you think you can be cured
she says

well hell yes, there must be some way I say
but you always seem to drink
when the affliction hits she says

yes I say
the drink seems to help it come out

like a waterfall in the spring
sided by stiff moss
but soft to touch like a woman's skin
smelling like a brand new sepia sandalwood
newspaper you have not read
but know already what it says inside

ok ok she says I get the picture

do phrases come to you upon sleeping
she says

yeh that's the worst time
I say

do you ever get images
in your mind she says
yeh, all the time I say

is it to do with authority she says
hell, everything's to do with authority I say

you don't like authority she says
hell, I just ignore authority I say

how did you feel as a kid she says
little I say

do you think your affliction comes from pain
she says

yeh drunk pain, love pain, grief pain
maybe they're the same pain I say

I mean we are the only animal that knows
it will die, apart from elephants I say

has it to do with conforming she says
yeh conforming stinks I say

are you worried about love she says
hell yes I say love is suffering

love is pain

love is dreaming about the same
person every night

even though you have been apart
for 24 years

always dreaming the same type of dream
like she was dead and you want her back

but the dream keeps on saying the same thing
that no matter how much you dream
the love is a spent force
between the two of us
while also screaming

you miss her
like you will miss breathing

so the two of you were close she says
for eight years we were like Bonnie and Clyde
on a crime free love spree, inseparable
like fish and chips with
salt and vinegar I say

apart from when she
went over to Russia I say

so what happened she says
she wasn't happy with my affliction I say
so she realized she says

yeh, but it had not gone fully blown
by that time I say
fully blown she says

fully blown I say
so I let her go I say

you let her go she says
she used to wear these gloves
these black lacy gloves I say

black lacy gloves she says
yeh I say

electric orange soul

the soul wanes,
the art appears

like
an electric
orange.

the only thing you
can really lose
is your
self.

I am you.
I am a yo yo.
I am yours.

I used to be a can can dancer
until I discovered jars.

blank minds
dig ego,

eager easter ego hunt.
(watch it go)

dig
blank ego
minds.

be free or still.
or still free.

the good dog laps
at life
the bad dog...

happy easter ego
happy ego?

16th century.
432.
124.
indian
blank slate minds.
feast.
aramaic.

easter ego hunt.

hell
is other people.

help is
other
people.

people are hell,
but it's all we got!

rat a tat tat.
snivel shit?

red injuns circle my
skin cells.

death shop chat

went to shop for death today, asked what they had.
well...we are offering a special today
blink and you'll miss it death

it's half price, but be quick or you'll miss it.
we have all the old favs, death by poison, sin,
sinful death,

that's suicide, which is on the cheap side.
short and sweet, sweet and sour death,
but you'll have to be drunk
in a takeaway for that one.

death in a breeze, bad wind
or whilst breaking wind.

death surrounded by loved ones,
that can be pricey as we might need actors.

death from a great height, small height
or no height at all.

death by socks, evil plastic bags,
coat hangers, oranges
or blue chairs coming at you, in a panic haze.

death in hospital, but that can be pretty lonely,
and they don't bother to feed you
if you are very old.

heart attack death, that's if you like surprises.
cancer death, but it can be nasty, long, drawn out.
death with the one you lurve
for romantic Smiths fans!

death while singing hymns during a confessional.
death in a car or on a bicycle

or while reading a poem out loud,
but it costs extra as we have
to supply a half decent poem.

death while taking in Bukowski, Monty Python,
Magnus Mills, Nirvana, Joy Division, Tindersticks
or the Sex Pistols, Stranglers, Clash and
Doestovsky.

death whilst doing the washing up
or watching noel edmonds,
that can be bloody nasty.

death whilst talking to a friend
on the phone about what death means.

death on the toilet,
reading a book about how death does not exist.

death whilst in the bath,
if you would like a clean death.

death whilst dreaming of death, that's a favourite.
death whilst drunk or sober, but you will probably
wish you had been drunk if you had been sober.

death with a dog or cat or with a cat and dog
or when it's raining them, but that's double.

death after you look at people
and their own sad loneliness,

like characters in a McCullers novel.
death when there is a faint birdy mist,
and you can hear and see them twittering.

funny happy death, which is more expensive,
takes lots of training.

death in war, cheapest we offer,
you can even get two for one.

death due to malnutrition, but you would
have to move to the third world or be in poverty.

when younger, all I thought of
was really doing it every day.

I told him I'd have a good think about it,
just didn't think I was quite ready for it yet.

he suggested I started saving up for it,
get some once in a lifetime training in

for our final ending shindig
that goes on forever
and a day.

looking out, at the inner outside of things

sat in the small trendy cinema café.
a woman who had been sitting to the right of me

came over to the other side of me by the window,
looked out and let out little squealing noises

cooey cooey in nature
whilst waving her arms about.
when she sat back down I looked out the window,

saw a bus with grim faces on it, all looking forward,
caught in the utter strangeness of the ordinary,
could not see anyone looking over at me.

as this happened a young girl was about to sit down
to the left of me, but maybe it was me looking over
to see who

the woman had waved at
which made it look like I

was looking over to the young girl
who carried a little leather case
which I guess

carried some form of musical instrument,
maybe a recorder and although I was looking past
and through the young girl she must have thought

I was looking at her in a strange
looking through you sort of way

like she was a ghost to me,
because she did not take the seat but went over
to sit by the window waiting for her two friends.

in the paper I read how ten hundred toy ducks and
ten hundred white trainers had been left floating in

some ocean after the ship sunk
and had started coming a shore somewhere.

all the ducks were now ghostly white
I had a picture in my minds eye

of a lonely fisherman
going out early morning on

some deserted misty beach
and suddenly coming across

the white ducks and trainers.
being surrounded by them in the silent grey stillness

probably wondering if he was imagining things
and looking up at the brooding sky

perplexed, as anyone could ever be
looking out at the inner, outside of things.

lurve

to laugh
you have to cry a little.

to lurve
you have to hurt a little.

to smile you
have to grin a little.

that's the feeling
that's the feeling
of
lurve.

to lurve you have
to be successful a big lot.
to lurve you

have to be
a multi millionaire
a little.

that's the feeling
that's the feeling of lurve.

to lurve you have to be
not old
and grey
and a bit too fat

and a bit of a loony
a little.

that's the beauty
that's the beauty of
love.

face down and fallen

she lay face down on the pavement
the medics were there

onlookers on looked whispering
dirty drunk, disgraceful, well I never

she did not move and was youngish
this was all some people witnessed
an end result, that pavement kiss

they did not see beyond the pavement
they did not see the woman

the woman battling against the role expected
to be feminine,

not to want more than a husband a kid
and a new kitchen

they did not see how her parents had fucked her up
good and proper, a job well done

they did not see her
being told to eat at a different table,
as if she had a contagious disease.

they did not see the circles run around her
from work, family

so as it all became too much, the living of a lie
having a different face for everyone

started as a way of coping, then became a reality
she forgot even existed
they did not see all this

they did not see her forced into a role
like a rag doll cut up and squeezed into a Barbie
they did not see the doctors

giving her this pill, then that pill, then this pill
for her to use to get high or slow
then deny her it

they did not see the education denied
because she never fitted in

to their narrow-minded corridors
they did not see how others only wanted to help

to give themselves a gold star
rather than her.

they did not see her walking the streets
almost insane from it all,
relationship after relationship.

they did not see some drunken bum opportunist
talk to her so kindly as she sat on the bench
half dead from it all.

they did not see him
use and abuse her then spit her out
because she talked back too much

they did not see this.
only her face down on the pavement,
a drunken bum.

but of course they only wanted to help
only to help,

they did not linger to see if
she was alive and kicking

they only wanted to help, to get their gold star
then be on their way to forget

they did not see
her pain, history or hurt.

just a drunken bum
alive and still kicking,
against the pricks.

come on I'm skint

it's funny,
the guy who sells books and assorted at the
flea market

always shouts out:
THREE BOOKS FOR A POUND
OR FIFTY PEE EACH

COME ON I'M SKINT!
GET DIGGING INTO MY STALL
BARGAINS!
BARGAINS!

BARGAINS!
COME ON I'M SKINT!

DON'T BE SHY
YOUR MUM WASN'T!

as I was looking at the books on his stall
someone said next to me
JESUS!
HE'S ALWAYS BLOODY SKINT!

and
I
agreed.

he always said
he
was

skint.

like it was
never ending.

like in real
life.

after buying a
number of books,

I became
skint
as well.

I just hope
it made him
happy.

although
I would never shout
about it,

like
him.

I had some
pride
left.

shop front face, laughing

it was a cold day, drizzling, late spring.
I got my coffee and sat down.

in front of me I could see the back of a
bald headed man
although not his face

having not noticed his face when I entered
I wondered if he had one
well, you never can be too sure.

a young mum sat to the side of me with a toddler
explaining to the waitress what school
she wanted to send him to.

noticed big grey patches of moisture
on the cafe's front window
looking out onto the street.

and at the top of the window
of the shop opposite

the word "HEATWAVE"
in bold black letters on red.

I clicked my camera twice.
no one appeared to notice or laugh.

I never did check if he had
a face.

culpitt wokey matters

death
is the same as
being in a shut

tight cardboard box
with packing tape
covering it

so as there is no
light.

the box is wrapped
in foam

so as sound
hardly gets through

and comes through muffled.
sentences come through as

dooobyy wobbby
culpitt wokey matters

you can not
move

speak
shout
complain.

if this death could be sold
they would make a packet

no law suits
complaints
or money back guarantees.

I have
seen the living

like this
version of death

never complaining
or kicking up a fuss.

just keep still
and shut

up
they say

to the kid,
they're breeding!

it's strange travelling

on the way back up
a man sat diagonally across from me.

the biggest black man you could ever see,
eating a chocolate bar.

I expected him to stand up and roar any second,
super hero like.

answering his phone he said he would get straight
onto it as soon as he'd left the train.

I pictured him flying off to some disaster.
then waiting on the platform

I notice business suited man
in waiting room with a hands free mobile phone.
I thought he was mad and talking to himself at first.

twenty years ago he'd have been locked up.
he came out of the waiting room

still talking to himself
"…the deal could be on, they need a decision by
3pm or it's off. Now look! I don't care if it's off,
I just need a decision from you, we could still go for
it…"

he carried some posh bags,
probably a new suit or shoes
and wandered up and down the platform

talking to himself, he even seemed to enjoy it.
then a train came in and someone asked me
if it was Birmingham?

I don't know I said
and he got on and asked and then got off
and the next time I saw him
he was on the platform opposite

looking into a timetables booklet
like he'd been doing on my platform.

then on the train this black kid in pram opposite me
seemed to enjoy looking into my eyes
and I enjoyed looking into hers.
because, kids never can lie.

and there was this half Alsatian dog
on the other side of us,

lying down and standing up nervously
at all the strange noises and judders.
ears all lopsided and the kid started
looking at the dog and I started looking at the dog
and the dog started looking at me and the kid
and it alternated between the three of us
but the dog got most of the looks from the kid
and the kid seemed more interested in the dog
and the dog seemed more interested in the kid

and I started feeling pretty damned
left out of things and looked at the moving
video like colour images going by outside

wondering, how I could ever feel jealous of a dog.
maybe the dog had not seen as many kids as me

or that's what I put it down to and tried to shrug off
the feeling of being left out of things,
again.

local news item

disability living allowance payments
are being stopped, re-named and cut.

one computer test
does not take into account how they are
or could be certain days,
mental ill health wise.

another is,
can you move this pen,

sit up and walk in a straight line,
brush your teeth in an orderly fashion.
say yes sir no sir, three bags full sir.

a man explodes himself to bits
in his cheap car

on some isolated, small country road in the
drizzling rain.

people say he kept himself to himself,
the newsagent said he visited
but not very often,

seemed pleasant, never said too much.
although he said he had looked
worried recently.

the newsagent was the star witness
to the guy's life.

no one knew his name, as he hardly ever spoke
or even said boo to a goose or ghost.

police said he had had mental health,
wipe away the pain and tears, tissue issues.

was working as a volunteer in a charity shop
but perhaps could do that no longer
as he had to find full-time paid work
that is not there anyway.

they said he did his bit for the local community
and this think big, big, small-minded society.

they said he was not planning to hurt anyone else,
from the suicide note they found in his flat.

they did not read out the suicide note
but they never do
do they.

they said they were not sure where he had
bought the home made explosives

a garden centre perhaps,
on special offer two for one.

they never said if he had had an
appointment for the new
disability non-mindful test

or had gone to one
and maybe been rejected as

not having
any mental health disability.

they never really said anything about
the new can you sit up straight,

say yes sir, no sir, three bags full sir,
disability tests.

but they
never do,
do they.

Faye King alien

see her every Faye King where!
with her alien Faye King hat on,
matching t-shirt and jacket.
with Faye King wings on all of them!
so she must be a Faye King alien!
she never wears anything else.
like an alien Faye King uniform!
like she's starting a Faye King
we are a winged hat Faye King alien school!
bet she thinks she's a Faye King god!
or a super human flying person!
and she's always Faye King miserable!
at the Sunday market, Metro station, Metro centre.
like she doesn't give a damn about being
not of this Faye King world!
she gets my Faye King goat up proper!
so Faye King fed up here!
like she thought it was going to be
a bed of Faye King roses!

always got her Faye King alien bouncers around her
seems to have a few bob.
why don't she get a Faye King taxi everywhere!
no, she likes to show off!
like, oh look at me with my
Faye King friends and money
and I'm a Faye King alien an'all.
don't we Faye King know it missus!

but her with her winged Faye King hat!
from another Faye King planet and she's

so Faye King pissed off just being here!
well missus, so are Faye King we!
what's she got to be so pissed off about?
she musta known what it would be like!
so why the hell she come here?
we don't need her sort here!
thinking she's Faye King alien royalty!
with her Faye King winged Faye King hat!
what's she got to be so Faye King pissed of about!
why don't she go Faye King back!
we Faye King can't!
why don't she Faye King fly away!
we can't even afford the Faye King bus fare!
or Faye King suicide with all the
Faye King trimmings!

poem for the lonely

cheer up
and
get
some
friends
or even
another
lurve

to
smile
and
laugh
with.

upon
death
you
will
not
be
able

to do
that
sort
of
gubbins
for
rather
a

long
time.

think
an
eternity

multiplied
by a zillion endless eternities
of boring sundays.

everyone
is
not
just an old/young
arsehole
like
me

with dribble
for
words
and inner lurve.

some
people
even
matter.

and can even
make
a fool
like me

feel
worthwhile
and happening.

as if lurve and feeling
had
never
even
gone
away

for
a
long
holiday

in
its inner

sun
shine.

lady death visits JJ's and discusses time management

having an all day breakfast
lady death sits opposite,

orders soup and tea
with furry fury hat
and shopping trolley.

the soup comes,
she sits and looks at it.

hey lover boy! lover boy!
oh Jesus! Jesus! feel like death,

bleedin flue init and I had the jab
fat lot of good that did!
just can't eat or drink no more,
just can't do it.

well I say, you have got to eat!
well yes... but all I do now is sit
and stare at the four blank walls

no visits, no one visits no more,
I can hardly breathe!
they've all got it too, so they don't visit no more.

I'm sorry... that's tough I say, wondering
if they were just plain scared?

oh Jesus, oh my gawd! do you want me tea?
no.. no... it's ok...really!

have to be at supermarket now, got appointment
always appoint-bloody-ments!

and she picked up her scythe and black hooded cape
and plodded wearily out of JJ's.

had a feeling I was lucky she only offered me tea
maybe, it was the sympathy?

maybe that...
saved me.

satisfyingly strong

on cider bottle
it says
in quotations
as though expressed
by a literary expert
a professor maybe
or don at Oxford
"satisfyingly strong"
in quotations
as though they went out
on the sidewalks
to ask someone young,
half dead through it,
"so, how does it feel?"
"satisfyingly strong, my good man,
call me a deathbulance,
my good man,
quick now, hurry to it,
me livers packed up,
by gods".

comin up tommy trinder-you lucky peoples!

why does thou so speaketh
the way of angels has gone!

and so it shall come to pass that those in the know
get biggy and fatty and lose their very senses!

and we must sure foot trot down and lay in naked
fields like the very butt of the camel
naked king shop fitter and yawning.

thou he does speaketh here and here
for the voice is everywhere like a camel's back

knitting needles pining for goodness
thou shalt not have
a merry making and stuff the hay!

my back like the sure footed scagg ass cement
buyeth of builders with brainy brawn and muscle

they hang their silver trinkets on
like a saw tooth fairy who can't knit any more!

with gladness the ripe ye shall yield to the
very purpose of toys r us.

the plain way ahead is unmarked but
leadeth the way to a stir fry a comeuppance!

for capitalist we all be – a sinin and a reekin
and capitalists have shiney teeth in their very mouth

speaketh like the very devil upturned and grinning
an unpleasant gawd awful smell.

to go backwards thou shalt hear the very voice of
the foot fetish toe fairy dragon
and marmalade soup on sundays.

let thee be blind and hear all that have cometh
thy way before heron addicts for fishes are their

king fairy dragons and hell fire on mountain top
bigger than sherbert dip lemons.

thy know thy fate as sundays gather pace,
the king toe nail fairy dragon is all a lose
and know thou shall not fear the dragons way!

go meekly unto the nite and buy your sixpences
well fart they shall be your last,
oh king dragon slayer.

thy sell Black Jacks in the place
you fear to go a treadin

and sings songs of praise every day the light shineth
and strikes ye down!

come yonder and peck at butts
like a mad pigeon looking

yonder for food and grey treacle for mind
and healing and be gone!
be gone I say, I say, I say.

for all that tread on treacle will be swearing uncouth
words of their camel back sofa king

and light fittings and flatty screeny tv's
that say the word is did and gone.

she looked over

she looked over, sensing the look
(we can all do this but most have forgotten)
looked back over. could only see someone
trying there best to fit in,
look like everyone else.
I was tired
it was not a dream.
my face showed it
not disgust or contempt.
just there would be no connection.
she read this, looked away jilted.
there wasn't any wonder in her eyes
wonder who I might be,
just the look I'd give you one.
like she'd become as hard as her men
over the years.
like swaying with no motion.
it's good to try and put the spark back anyhow
and takes some doing,
now I need mine putting back.
it was like having
two different TV's close up
on different channels
with the sound down,
plugged in
but not connected.
could she have saved me?
could I have saved her?
as if secret lovers
with a hidden purposeful
meaningful lurving intent.

someone sometimes, a part of nothing going nowhere without everyone

with nobody.
no more a part of this than
a lone tree in a woodless burnt out wood.

never go anywhere,
come back from anywhere.

tramp like a lone
penny whistle looking for

an idle less song
about lost lurve, grief and sorrow,
sad songs are best.

mosey about,
a fish looking for a salty sea.

any sea,
even a dried up dead one.

read the Gronad,
know what's happening,
in our little worlds.

my world, your worlds.
the only world we will have,

together
just this once,
a life times blink of a blink.

kick up a fuss
stand firm
make a difference

protest,
a true punk, inside your inner battle.

everyone should be
someone.

write it all down
if you have to.

we only get a smudge, wink
of a chance.

we can't all
be
no one.

someone has to be someone
or it would be boring,
wouldn't it?

sometimes nothing ever happens,
nothing happening is something.

if you, at heart
remember you can be,

someone,
sometimes.

sleep

think
sleep
is a
pretend run
and practice
on death
to get
you used to it
before
it
happens
for
real.

the all new samaritans

job centre staff have
been informed how to deal
with suicide threats

and question if they should be being
re-trained to be Samaritans,

and know now
if a suicide threat
is genuine or not.

they have been given magic glasses
from India
blessed by holy men in turbans and loin cloths

to see someone's true karma around them
and so can tell by its colour and smell,
if the threat is serious or not.

and if to contact emergency services
and cliff top tourist places

lighthouses and life boat services.
this could save a lot of money
they reckon,
in the long run and big drop,

save money
on
false
emergencies

and naughty people
fibbing about
how ill they are

inside their now
almost empty soul mind lighthouses

so that they can no longer do voluntary work
for MIND.

the birds

kids coming flying out of the library.

earlier saw
one of them chucking
out DVD's of the
DVD show holders,
onto the floor.
flinging them all out
like they were angry with them
just for being DVD's in a library setting.
which was kind of funny
in an anarchic way.

so they come out and make
indeterminate movements
like birds and arrive
on a small section
of Hadrian's wall.
and act like it's
bird victory
day.

and I am smiling
inside
because it is so funny
and life affirming.

and life sure is
short of that
sort of stuff
at present.

because I
get drunk some
nights and sometimes puke.
and play my music loud or not?
as sometimes I cannot remember if I have.

which can make it even
worse
for
me.

and I start to wish
I was a bird like them
and could fly

away
with another bird
to make a

Hadrian's Wall
bird victory day nest.

the gates of hell and the blue balloon

two dogs
as fierce as a
tunundra waterfall

stood guard by
the gates,
going down.

someone came with pram,
the push chair not the overlooked group
with a blue balloon tied on to it, floating above.

one of the dogs
tried to smell
the blue balloon.

as their
snout touched
and nudged

both the balloon
and hound darted back.

the hound jumped up
pulling at the lead,

causing everyone to be alarmed,
then laugh about it.

it made me feel
easier about things.

53

at least I wasn't
afraid of a
blue balloon.

I knew
we were all going
down.

why do they need security here!
if they don't let in drinkers

who will they let in,
even with a blue balloon.

I'd figured it out,
all I needed was a blue balloon!

or it was all a con
and I was really going up
instead of down.

the invisible kid

I am the invisible kid
with or without the many old bandages,
I have accumulated.

old age makes you invisible,
it's good for not being noticed
and bad for getting seen by the
young and the beautiful but not normally gifted.

maybe, only the old are gifted?
they have been through it all, many times!

wearing hats is good for my self esteem
it covers grey hairs
and helps when you can't afford
a cheap five pound punky short and spiky haircut.

often feel like I don't exist,
that's probably why I get drunk and arrested,
when I stick my two fingers up at the police,
as they have treated me badly sometimes.

the young don't know what they have
until it's gone, bled and burnt out of them.

or they do it to themselves
with slippers, sheds and too much
apple pie goodness.

I was brought up from three to seven
by my grandmother Pud,

in a small Brighton bed and breakfast
hotel for thespians

it was haunted, Pud would see and hear a man.
I saw Victorian couples with parasols
out on the balcony

in the shadow moving car street lights
and heard witches cackling,
my brother saw roman soldiers marching through.

I thought robbers and criminals became policemen
and men turned into women,
my mind had not worked out sex and birth.

I self harmed with a razor
on my face many times once,
it healed quickly.

I was annoyed at being ignored,
after coming back to the family fold,
after many years away.

hid in a closet cupboard one day,
my family were looking for me
my mother went spare,
until they found me, curled up.

Pud would exclaim what the heck
would Richard want to do with the ladies!
like it was a non thought!
still makes me smile.

my English teacher, Mrs English
made me read The spy who came in from the cold
I wrote an essay on it and got top marks!

I thought Star Trek would be my future
and planned to become an astronaut
and visit the moon.

when six or seven
I visited a naughty older kid,
who's parents owned the local food shop.

as no one was around,
he got us both to stand naked
in front of a big mirror.

we looked perplexed at the strange dangling things,
we both seemed to each have an identical copy of.

as a kid on holiday
in a caravan I got up in the night
to piss in a bucket

which became
next mornings tea for my elder brothers
who noted the strange taste,

but gulped it all down.
it became known as the wee tea experience.

they still blame me for it,
and have never been the same since!

as a kid my eldest brother bet me
I would not take Tippy my dog
around the block in a multi coloured tank top,
I won the bet and got funny bemused looks.

as a kid we only had one book,
about a ghostly ship lost and floating at sea

where people had turned to ghosts,
it had pictures in it,
my sister remembers it too.

don't think I believe in anything
apart from grief, lurve, change, sacrifice, healing,
re-birth, co-operation, feeling, will power
and the soul's ability at self renewal,
being a true Joseph Beuys fan.

would not have completed the fine art degree
without Joseph
and his many felt, wax
and mad march hare happenings.

I regret I never met Charles Bukowski and Joseph
and forget why I made my mother smile and laugh
out aloud

on the way back from church
aged around eleven,
think it had something to do with
religion or bankers?

she is not here to ask, anymore.

maybe all we become,
is an ill tuned memory

and the next line of invisible lost ghosts,
waiting forever and a day

to be
seen and heard,
again.

the lady and the dog

on the moving train the black Labrador stands
tongue hanging out, taking in the moving
all new colour pictures outside.

wonder if he realises why they
seem to be moving and at such speed.

the sky is blue with clouds, we enter a tunnel
the dog looks puzzled

at the thick blackness of the outer outside.
the train stops a man gets off
the dog stares at him like he's a new friend

come to play and tries to edge closer to him
to smell him check him out,
find out where he's been.

then it lays down. the dog's owner
puts her hand down, tries to pat the dog's head

not realising he is lying down.
feel sad she can not stroke his smooth head.
the lady is clinging onto a pole in the centre.

next stop, she peers outside,
unable to see the place signs

as though trying to look through a heavy mist,
I wonder if I should tell the lady what stop it is

but someone with a suitcase on wheels tells the lady
the dog has a mighty sniff of the
lady's suitcase and dress.

we all wait patiently for the lady with the black dog
to get off first

and someone else has words
with her concerning where she needs to go next

"I've got a ticket already" she says.
feel amazed at how good people can be

wonder how I could ever cope with not
seeing things, places and people,
she must be very brave.

wonder if anyone ever fully realises what they have
and decide, most do not, just take it for granted.

later I see an eye catching woman
just standing in the street talking to someone,

feel like going up
and simply saying you are beautiful but do not

I'm the shy type, but not as bad as I used to be.
remember again how lucky I am

to see beautiful women, blue skies with clouds
and black dogs with their tongues hanging out,
like their smiling.

if the black dog could have talked to me
he would probably have said
"what did you see, smell and hear today, buster"

the bag of bones man

there's a guy I see around the same age as me
maybe younger, but he looks older
with mental health issues, as thin as a rake
ill fitting clothes due to shrinkage

I see him around the city centre
recently he had many months beard on him
hair that was wild and long that had not been cut
or washed for months

just going up to people and saying he had not eaten
for five days and can they spare any change
I often see him just sitting at the bus stop

up the road, not waiting for a bus
he just sits there as thin as a rake
waiting for nothing to ever happen
for the best anyhow

maybe he failed the Atos test
or has to pay the bedroom tax
due to being unable to move

saw him at a city centre bus stop as thin as a rake
his body was twitching, his right arm would fly up
like a Nazi salute, as if he couldn't help himself
and then lower and then he would rub his mouth

as if he couldn't help it and this was repeated
many times like a cartoon man
stuck on repeat as if he couldn't help it

until the bus came

to take him god knows where?
maybe a psychiatric ward
just a bag of bones, twitching involuntarily
on repeat public performance mode

he used to get food on tick
from the newsagent who was a kind man
but he retired a while back

so that safety measure is not there anymore.
wish I had filmed the twitching man at the bus stop
to show the tory coalition

just
what
they
are
doing to
a lot of people

it will not save any money
as the bag of bones man will
be back in psychiatric hospital soon probably
and may never leave there

due to idiot millionaire MP's
trying to skin people
whilst they are
still just about alive
just to save them cash
which it will not anyway

in the long run.

his hope, feelings, independence, self esteem, pride
and personality
wiped out as if by magic

just another beggar bag of bones man
bothering you again and again for small change
any change would do

like a sad song you can not get out
of your head on continuous repeat
public performance
day in
day out.

recently he was sitting on a bench
shouting out "come my friends help me "
shoppers walked a distance away from him

as if he had a contagious decease
they could not get out of their head

is this the way we should treat people
who maybe need a little help?

it's inhumane, cleansing the poor
and or disabled of any hope.
maybe they will even bring back the work house?

another preventable suicider waiting to happen
in his and your lifetime

it's the only one he and we get,
just this once
this one shot.

the looker

she was sitting diagonally across from me
on the metro.

had a Harry Potter book on her lap
and an old faded denim jacket lined for cold times
and a guitar in case.

long brown hair, it was her mouth that grabbed me,
so thin and delicate.
went down a little at the sides, not like frowning.

it was angular, an angular mouth
along with her angular eyebrows
that went up in the middle,
like a hill I longed to climb again,

just the way she moved, picking up the book,
just the way she got to know
the vacant still air better.
20 to 25.

the way she slid through it.
the way she sat and thought.
sat and looked out the window.

wished I could have done something.
recognized something in her angular features

she briefly noticed me.
the man with the black walking stick.
the man so taken aback.

I could do nothing.
currently, I am beaten.

that time on the metro
made it all worth it, made the day worth it.

even though I could do nothing
but admire a reflection
of someone I recognized, inside out.

the meeting

yeh, I went to see the psychiatrist recently.
last meeting never happened.
he had blanked me in the street.
I wanted to ask him what was happening
about the meeting.
he just blanked me and
talked into his mobile,
secret things and words.
then at the new meeting,
I asked him why he had blanked me out
in the street.
very hush hush he said,
I work for a secret gov organisation
he said
very hush hush.
I am their top operative,
he said.
one day we will take over the world
he said.
is it a criminal related biss I asked?
yes, he said and I can say no more
very hush
hush
he said.
I have super powers he said,
very hush hush.
you might have
blown my cover.

the poet

there's a man, lives in my street
who lowers the tone of the neighborhood.
me dad says so.

he lives on his own and wears fifties suits
without a tie, which is a bit odd

always looks like his mind is elsewhere
on holiday, somewhere raining, maybe.
which is bit odd.

and does not work and does not even own a car
just a cheap tatty bike
which is bit odd.

he even plays classical music and sings to himself
sometimes, which is very very odd.

I know he lowers the tone because I've seen him
going out, furtively, in a big black coat
and black woolly hat in the small hours

cycling to the neighborhood tone volume dial
at the end of our street.

he turns it right down, the blighter!
when everyone's asleep and not looking.

see sparks fizzing from diodes
hear a distant crackle and hum
and crazy man laughter.

me dad says, they should keep it padlocked
or house prices will plummet,

which is not very odd,
but understandable, really.

the seagull

a seagull was at the window
looking into the hospital,
as my mother lay dying.

it moved from the left to right,
closer and closer to my mother.

seemed to be looking in on how humans die,
love and grieve.

had a prozac dream last night,
a seagull was outside,

I pressed my hand up against the pane,
as though I could feel its feathers, through it.

the seagull as if knowing this
pressed its body up against the glass

as if it wanting me to touch it, feel it,
feel its living feathers.

maybe it was seeing the seagull
as my mother lay dying

that lodged in my mind, as an image of death
waiting, watching.

my mother is now someplace else
where I can not touch her

or see her flying as free as a sleepless bird,
as free as the last death.

toward the end of the dream the seagull put its wing
through a crack in the window, a small gap
and I touched its long wings.

it was like touching death
and feeling its flapping wings
trying to escape, trying to come home.

as if my mind could finally
feel the reality of the situation.

the reality of death along with its beauty.
it was as though the glass that separated us
was not just physical but mental

as I have not cried yet, the funeral is still to come.
I pray and hope that I will cry then,
even with my prozac mind.

feel very alone, because she was always there,
no matter what the hell
I was going through, always there.

if I could put my mothers love into a box
it would be Tardis like

there would be some winning betting slips,
red wine included

along with lots of love, hope, empathy and humour

and a strong desire
for a better world,
still to come.

the toilet incident

In the city looking in a charity shop for some books to give as presents found CARSON McCULLER'S, THE HEART IS A LONELY HUNTER which is something I want to give to family and friends, so had to get it. As walked to counter I felt a huge surge down below and walked in a very amusing way to counter and prayed they could serve me at once, so as I could go to a toilet. They did and I had white linen trousers on I noticed that showed any kind of wetness up immediately and glaringly and wondered what hell would do if shit pants and how embarrassing it would be. Stood at side of counter holding legs together, doing a kind of shimmy still dance. Praying I could keep it in until book were given to me. Then ran to the nearest gents. Angry when people got in my way. Someone noticed the anxious look on my face and I looked at them and thought, Christ, I hope you never feel like I do. People seemed to be acting like they were out for a Sunday stroll. I was just about to shit self with the wrong sort of pants on that would show it all up, big time. It was about honour. Prayed a toilet would be vacant and one seemed to be, although closed. Pulled down my easy-to-see-if-liquid-has–been-spilled–on–them-linen-fashion-pants and prayed I was in time. The pulling down of the easy-to-see-if-you-have-shit-yourself–pants caused a chain reaction and I prayed it would not make it to the trousers that were easy-to-wear-comfort–linen-pants that showed up big time if you shit yourself. Had had diarrhoea problems since taking up drink as a hobby. The dark liquid poured into my knickers and the floor and the walls and the toilet and everywhere. It was like an atom bomb or me deciding humanity was not really for me. I prayed don't hit the trousers and looked down at my knickers, shoes, coat, belt and everywhere. My easy-to-spot-diarrhoea-sufferer–trousers thankfully had seemed to be spared. I thought there must be a god and hoped it was a woman as most men and I definitely stunk when we had bad days out. In and out of hospital. And I wished for hospital and not public humiliation with my mental health issues. Started clearing up hoping the toilet paper would last. My knickers were unwearable and could not work out how I would take them off and put them in bin outside without being seen. Had to think quick like a spitfire pilot under attack by nazi scum. I worked out that I had to get my shoes off and then easy-to-see-if-you–have-shit-yourself-comfort-linen-trousers. Then I could maybe get the pants off. I worked out that I would need to clean all the shit up from the floor in order to stop it from transferring to my trousers when I pulled them down and off. But could not work out how I would carry the knickers to the bin without being seen or smelled? Subversion I thought, trick them or maybe some form of subliminal hypnosis. Then a loud voice let out, *You had an accident Mr?* Yes, I replied but I don't really want to discuss it in a public environment. *I'll give you some spray and extra toilet paper.* Thanks I said, had run out of paper a long time ago. He threw them over the door, over the locked prison I was in and said *Make sure you clean it all up!* Yes, I replied. My body's giving up! Nothing's working right. The blood puke, getting banned, the toilet problems that can not be spoken of. I must be cursed I thought, he's telling me have I had an accident like I was a two year old not able to hold anything in, this feels like regressing! I had come up with a plan about the knickers, wrap them in toilet paper, maybe if I did it quick, people would not see. So I cleaned up with the flower spray goodness and figured it would take me 15 seconds to make it to the bin. I went out like a French resistance fighter thinking don't see my dirty pants and someone came by and I'm not sure if they saw my shit pants and I put them into the bin. And washed my hands many many times, as if I had just got infected with a bad case of the OCD virus. Thinking what I went through in the name of getting THE HEART IS A LONLEYHUNTER. But it was probably worth it, at least that was spared.

the magician

the baby sat in his pram
on the Metro

he started watching me,
trying to uncover how big my
soul measured perhaps or the colour of it

maybe even where I kept it
hidden and padlocked.

it seemed that the kid
liked what he had found

I looked over and gave
a quick smile

the kid smiled and
did this amazing little trick.

he held out both of his tiny hands
and raised them up
in front of him

to show me
he could do this
magic trick

then he put them back down
and smiled

and then he held them up again,
magic.

I smiled back
and the little kid seemed
mighty pleased with himself

and so did
I.

the shriek

the kid was standing over
the other side of the platform.

she was a young lady
there was something about her way.

she did not talk and her maybe Mother
went to the other side of her

and placed the young lady's right hand into
a pocket she had in her jacket.

maybe, because it had turned colder.
maybe, because she really cared.

you do not see that sort of thing
happening much now days.

and I wondered as she had not said anything
to her maybe mother.

it had all been done with eye contact
as far as I could see.

just wondered, if the lady had a learning difficulty.
and felt amazed

how much the maybe mother really cared about her
maybe daughter or maybe they were sisters?

then as the Metro train turned up.
The lady gave a little shriek of excitement
owhoooooooooooooooooooooooooo!

and it sounded really good
and I felt like giving a little shriek myself

as way of a reply, like an owl.
but I didn't

because people just
don't do that sort of thing

nowadays,
which is a crying shame.

upon waking up

woke up, I'd been at school
tried to go to a poetry club
but had mislaid my poetry.

I'd been trying to find it for a tutor,
an American, but could not find it.

at the poetry club was an ex girlfriend
although she didn't seem to know me.

I'd been reading a true life story about
someone who had a short time to live
the day before, maybe it was that.

I thought all this is temporary, my personality,
my ways, me and everyone else.

all very temporary, not the normal state of affairs.
we come from nothing, maybe end up as nothing.

so this little blip we get of life
is like something very temporary.

which makes all this pretty amazing:
views, smells, touch, longing, colour,
smiling, bowel movements, pissing, love (is a dog
from hell=BUKOWSKI), taste, feelings, rain,
clouds, wind, breeze, art, reading, black and white
films, friends, lovers, music, spirit, soul, booze,
laughing (when you can),
crying (when you can not).

like being the star actor in a grainy black and white
B movie
about our own life.

walking shells full of the stuff of dreams,
for a short period blink of a time.

death is eternal and forever
(two eyes will never meet two eyes again)

but we do need
the sharp bit at the
end (thank you Joseph Beuys)

to keep us awake,
alive and kicking.

more fragile than the dead

even after the funeral you don't believe it
the only time it really hit me
was when I was confronted with

the space

that was to be filled with my eldest brothers body
just seeing

the space

did it

maybe before also the phone call "He's dead"
that lasted around 2 minutes of grief
of trying to cry

I didn't get it anymore after that
even with the funeral and all

even with his friend throwing in a book
even with the funeral service playing Beatles

like he wanted them to "I want to hold your hand"
he had just got married with two kids

who would drink pub cokes
as we drank a little together

arguing about the merits of the Beatles
against the merits of Punk

the human condition
Joseph Beuys the late great artist said
(in a roundabout way)

through loss and grief humankind grows
(you could add sacrifice as well)

sociologists have a word for it
which means you can never grieve your own death
it's always left to others

that's you me and everyone down/up here
god must be an anti-capitalist
have a sense of humour

you can't buy grief
you can't buy life
the only one you can buy is death

sometimes people are kinder than kind
and funnier than funny

more fragile than the dead
it could make you cry buckets of grief

let it all out
twist and shout
twist and shout

my trails as Jesus Mark two

had a schizophrenic breakdown in 2003,
started hearing different voices talking to me

that were not real,
it was not because of drink
was not drinking much.

ended up thinking I was dead
or in heaven or purgatory.

over a two week period lost any sense of reality,
hardly ate or slept

had to get out
went to Tynemouth beach on the Metro.

don't know why?
hardly ever go there.

overhead a helicopter was hovering
like in a film noir

written in big letters on the sand
were the words
"HALO RICH"

and next to it
someone had drawn a big key.
my nickname at school had been Ackey

and whilst studying for a fine art degree

had done a huge piece
with many replica resin keys.

seeing my name and the key
made me flip
and still does thinking about it.

it is, was and will forever be inexplicable.
was it a message from my favourite brother Mark

who died in 2000 from throat cancer aged only 50?
he used to call me Rich.

or a message from
cocker spaniel
spelt backwards?

first took fifty six parecetomol
laid down to die on the bed,

ended up puking in
the toilet
the whole evening.

things got worse,
thought the voices were
going to hurt my family

so threw myself off my balcony
four flights up from Byker Wall.

thought it would stop
the voices hurting my family.

somehow landed with my fingers
on the hard concrete

the digits popped out of my fingers
and broke my leg,
the pain is indescribable

luckily did not land on anyone,
a kind man called an ambulance.

although I manage to ignore it
most of the time,

at the back of my mind
I wonder if I might be
Jesus Mark two

and my belief in god
is greater
but I think she

has long legs
and a
soft husky voice.

just call me birdman or kinda lucky,
I can see why people use the lift now.

size 12?

death comes in all shapes and sizes,
size 12 anyone?

toboggan run death, shoe shop death,
death whilst reading the morning papers,
death whilst feeling rain and wind on your face.

death on an open top bus
whilst listening to people say how good
or bad they feel about themselves and others.

death whilst hearing a secret, secret death,
heron addict watching death, lunatic death,
death under the moon, death on the news again.

death over cornflakes,
death with a pencil in your hand, death by pencil.

death under the stairs,
homeless death under the stars,
death to the other side,
death by rolled up newspaper.

death of silence, death of hearing, death of sight,
death of feeling, thought, free -will and purpose.
death of the best band you ever heard.
fence death. hedge fund manager death.

death of humor, death of laughter,
death in a silent black and white film,
death of poetry, death of thought,

death of seeing someone else smile,
like you might even be in love again, as if.

death of patting a dog on the head
and smiling at how crazy and free it looks,
death comes to presidents and prime ministers
the same as us.

the final full stop which is like a drug we use to
remind ourselves that all this is fleeting for us and
an eternity of nothingness like a blank blackboard
beckons us for ever and a day with no chalk lines.

Joseph Beuys called it the sharp bit at the end to
keep us all awake.
an eternity of being dead that is.

death of a planet, death of a tree, death of a stream,
death of an ice cap, death of a penguin,
death of a polar bear, do you really care?

death of determination, death of conviction, death
of caring, death whilst watching a great animation
by the QUAY BROTHERs

which made you feel like you were watching
someone else's dream.
and thought, hell! they must be pretty crazy too.

I just wrote this and my computer packed up and so
lost it all and re-wrote it from memory so this might
not be exactly the same poem

I had written and I have forgot half of what I wrote
because I am a little drunk but hell I must be still
alive, perhaps?

BUKOWSKI once wrote you can die
every night with drink

and wake up the next morning as though
risen from the dead!

and yes, I have died a few times
and sometimes wake up again
as though re-born.

the main thing about death is that you can never
re-boot this life again and all its
beauty, pain and sly grim humour.

you really are tazzled big time upon dying and no
one gets a second chance and all you hear forever is
friends and family crying buckets if you are lucky
or unlucky over a hailstorm of your
own lonely eternities.

making you wish you had kicked up a fuss
down/up here as if you had really cared
given a darn about anyone else other than yourself.

when things and damn shopping all get too much in lurve

busy Friday, people shopping in Oldham,
to find a false reason to continue not being.

notice man, he had her on the ground,
he was on top.

a girl kid stood by, finger on lips, not sure.
most pretended they couldn't see them,
too busy shopping anyhow.

the man, wearing an old beat up leather jacket
scruffy t-shirt, had her pinned down.

she made yelping sounds, hair strewn across face
tangled, web like, no features to see,
almost sobbing.

could only see one other grown up
viewing the tragic events.

then she lay on the ground, still.
the shifty short haired man

stood a bit away, sheepishly.
thumbs in jeans, head high.

trying to hide an evil looking grin.
pretending he had nothing to do

with the lady on the floor,
glancing at her occasionally.

then folded his arms
and plain ignored her like Euripides.
acted interested in the sale sale sale signs
across the way.

MUST be crazy I thought.
shoppers passed oblivious,
walking either side quickly.

no smiles on their straight jacketed laced up,
sewn up, clamped tight faces.

eventually, she got up,
straightened herself out, went over,
picked up the kid,

who still had a finger up to mouth
and poked the man in the stomach.

"Hell Henry, you KNOW I'm ticklish!
we'll sort it out.......somehow."

then they all laughed and
quit shopping, forever.

escaping out

all we are left with is a husk
some dead meat

something to be put finally away
at fifty

no matter
he made people lurve a little

brought them together to get
a little drunk and high

smile and laugh
so as it hurt

after meeting with him
and arguing
about the merits of the Beatles and Punk

all you remember
really remember

is
the way he laughed

he'd sit on his hands
and rock back and forth
and rub his beard

as though he was trying to
keep his laughter inside

stop it from escaping out

while banging his hand on the table
counting the human

heart
beats
to his laughter

maybe he was even trying to
pass it on

maybe that is really what he was
trying to do

not trying to do
but managing to do

very well
thank you very much

I miss him
one of a one off

he never got drunk
no matter how much he drank

his elderly ex priest teacher
wrote to my mother

that god will be very pleased
with his
new friend

dreams

so how are
your dreams
going?

mine are always
utter nightmares

but good ones
a passion cold sweat
about them

they wake me up
keep me thinking

and smoking
way into the night

and morning
about the plots

moves
and terrible acting.

like I was one of the
good guys

in Alias Smith
and Jones

the 70's cowboys,
remember.

why do I like drinking too much?

to get out of it
to forget
to remember
to feel
to feel numb, fit in or not fit in
to find my own non religious spirituality
to feel bliss
to deal with anger, negativity and rejection
to deal with grief, schizophrenia and alienation
to deal with or even make bi-polar happen again
to deal with a massive hole of insecurity inside
to help me to be creative or even sleep
to help me to cry or smile and laugh
to be a part of something
to rebel
to get high or low
to put two fingers up at everything and everybody
because of habit
because of no hope, job, career, lurve,
intimacy or feelings
because of an addiction I am addicted too
because of my lifestyle, peer pressure
and friends or lack of
because of a lack of a positive future
because of child hood, adolescent
and adult life trauma's
because of no positive role models early on
because of no real family that keep in touch
because I don't have an identity
because I am feeling nervous, on edge,
hopeless and depressed

because I self medicate due to mental illness
because I am feeling numb
because everything, everyone, my life
and life is bullshit
so as not to conform or even to conform
for an identity
to help me forget I once cared
to help me forget what I once remembered
and even loved.

zig zag death

it was a strange day, people walking into me
like I didn't exist.

I'd been to the flea market
looking in junk bins to see if I could come up

with anything to make life seem like
it was worth living again.

most of the time I did not feel like
continuing with nothing to show,
apart from a hangover, vomit on the floor.

having a smoke,
outside the Metro with a rucksack full of stuff

I hoped would
make me feel like continuing this

once in a lifetime fight
without the feeling of needing to put a halt to it.

an old lady came into my view, in front of me.
an eastern European immigrant

was playing his accordion
just to the side of me and it had heart and soul.

collecting pennies, you could tell he did it
because he loved it.

the lady had a long black coat
plastic bag and furry cat hat.

I could only see her back
but could tell she was getting on

by the way she walked and danced.
right in front of me she did a zig zag dance

with arms outstretched
like a bird waiting to take off.

she danced to the music,
zig and zagged in between sad shoppers

who tried to ignore her,
looking at her like she was insane.

it felt wonderful that she could do this,
not be locked up for doing it.

no one said or did anything about her apparent
lunacy. I was still in England.

she came close to a shop,
but zig zagged her way away from it.

she had a bag attached to her arms,
a gift to the gods maybe.

if I'd been near to death like her
I'd not give a monkeys what people thought,

if I'd lived a happy life, like she hopefully had
I'd like to show what life really meant.

maybe it's not just about money, shopping
or giving a jot how bad it can get.

perhaps at best, happy moments make up life,
when you do not care about
what anyone thinks of you

how much money you earn, what car you own
how many kids you have,
what places you go to escape living.

I'd had a fine time
picking up bric-a-brac for fifty pee

in an effort to keep on trying my best
not to die again.

the zig zag lady was a good sight,
 just trying to find a way,
a reason to carry on with this earthly living shindig.

she must be so close to copping it
that it didn't worry her anymore.
wished I could be like her too, unafraid of Dr.D

as if it was just a little cliché
to be overcome like life is.

the keys I am hitting sound like bullets going off
like a wake up call,
that sounds good.

sometimes, everything makes sense,
you can even smile
in wonder.

Bio

Richard was taught at an early age by nuns. He grew up in a haunted house and learned to read late. He trained to be a psychiatric nurse and also gained a Fine Arts degree in Liverpool. After reading Charles Bukowski in his early thirties, he started writing. He has been published a few times, most recently by Underground Books (New York). His YouTube site is known as "Lurvesoul" where videos of some of his art, poetry and radio broadcasts can be found. He attends the Brown Room poetry group and Scratch performance group monthly and can be seen performing at poetry open mics in and around Newcastle.

Lightning Source UK Ltd.
Milton Keynes UK
UKOW06f0147210315

248275UK00009B/92/P